and Diggers

Mary Kate Doman

Enslow Elementary

an imprint of

Enslow Publishers, Inc.

40 Industrial Road
Box 398
Berkeley Heights, NJ 07922
USA

http://www.enslow.com

For Liam, who loves things that go.

Enslow Elementary, an imprint of Enslow Publishers, Inc.

Enslow Elementary® is a registered trademark of Enslow Publishers, Inc.

Library of Congress Cataloging-in-Publication Data

Doman, Mary Kate, 1979–
  Earthmovers and diggers / by Mary Kate Doman.
      p. cm. — (All about big machines)
  Includes index.
  Summary: "Learn how construction vehicles are used every day"—Provided by publisher.
  ISBN 978-0-7660-3931-5
  1. Earthmoving machinery—Juvenile literature. 2. Construction equipment—Juvenile literature.
I. Title.
  TA725.D58 2012
  621.8'65—dc23
                                        2011014638

Paperback ISBN 978-1-59845-245-7

Printed in the United States of America

052011 Lake Book Manufacturing, Inc., Melrose Park, IL

10 9 8 7 6 5 4 3 2 1

To Our Readers: We have done our best to make sure all Internet Addresses in this book were active and appropriate when we went to press. However, the author and the publisher have no control over and assume no liability for the material available on those Internet sites or on other Web sites they may link to. Any comments or suggestions can be sent by e-mail to comments@enslow.com or to the address on the back cover.

♻ Enslow Publishers, Inc., is committed to printing our books on recycled paper. The paper in every book contains 10% to 30% post-consumer waste (PCW). The cover board on the outside of each book contains 100% PCW. Our goal is to do our part to help young people and the environment too!

Photo Credits: © 2011 Photos.com, a division of Getty Images. All rights reserved., pp. 6, 10–11, 14–15, 16–17, 18–19, 20–21, 22–23; Christian Lagerek/Shutterstock.com, pp. 4–5; Dmitry Kalinovsky/Shutterstock.com, pp. 12–13; MiloVad/Shutterstock.com, title page; nikkytok/Shutterstock.com, pp. 8–9

Cover Photo: MiloVad/Shutterstock.com

Note to Parents and Teachers

Help pre-readers get a jumpstart on reading. These lively stories introduce simple concepts with repetition of words and short simple sentences. Photos and illustrations fill the pages with color and effectively enhance the text. Free Educator Guides are available for this series at www.enslow.com. Search for the *All About Big Machines* series name.

Contents

Words to Know

around   away   tools

Earthmovers and diggers work hard.

They help with jobs
in town.

Bulldozers move dirt around.

A backhoe digs.

A paver rolls.

A crane lifts heavy tools.

A dump truck takes
rocks away.

Tractors push, pull, and plow.

There are a lot of jobs in town.

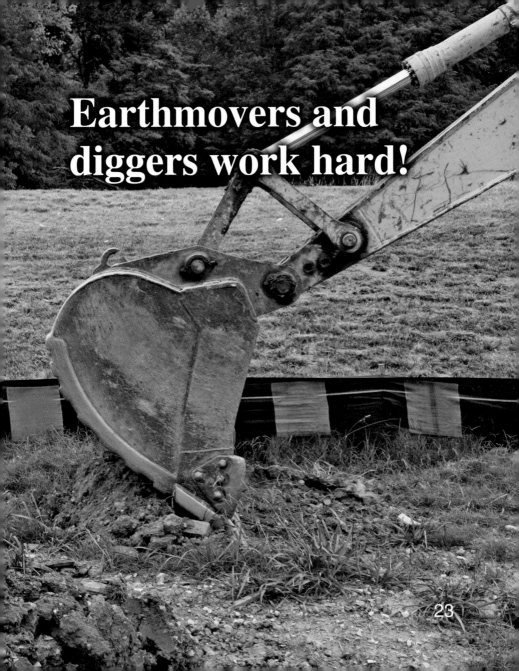

Earthmovers and diggers work hard!

Read More

Deschamps, Nicola. *Digger.* New York: DK Publishing: New York, 2002

Hill, Lee Sullivan. *Earthmovers.* Minneapolis: Lerner Publications, 2011

Williams, Linda D. *Earthmovers.* Mankato, MN: Capstone Press, 2005.

Web Sites

CBeebies Shows: Bob the Builder
<http://www.bbc.co.uk/cbeebies/bobthebuilder/games/>

National Geographic Channel: Earthmovers
<http://channel.nationalgeographic.com/series/ man-made/3798/Overview>

Index

Guided Reading Level: C
Guided Reading Leveling System is based on the guidelines recommended by Fountas and Pinnell.

Word Count: 50